You'll Die Laughin'

AUSSIE JOKES

Compiled and illustrated by Melva Graham

Copyright © Melva Graham, 2019

171 Blackjack Road, Harcourt Vic, 3453
Ph/Fax: 03 5474 2871

First printed, 2005
Reprinted, 2008, 2011

ISBN: 978-0-6481726-6-6

CONTENTS

A man isn't poor if he can still laugh.

Blokes 'n Sheilas
Singles / Cash-and-Carried 7

Bushies 19

Colder than a Mother-in-law's Kiss 30

Flesh-pressers 34

Funny Buggers, All of Us. 38

God-botherers 52

Limerick Lulus / Bush Wisdom 58

Medico Mirth 66

Muscle Bound Between the Ears
(and blonde on top?) 74

Naughty Naughties 84

Old Codgers. 93

Pissed as a Parrot. 98

Tight-arses 104

Tin Lids 108

Blokes 'n Sheilas
Singles / Cash-and-Carried

All men are alike, but they have different faces so you can tell them apart.

She's shy about telling people her age – about ten years shy.

When you're a young bloke, women tell you, "Look, but don't touch." As you get older, you hear the opposite.

Adam: "Honey, where's my pants?"
Eve: "We're having them for salad tonight."

Both my marriages have been disappointing. My first wife left me, and my second wife won't.

She's a great little housekeeper. Every time she gets divorced, she keeps the house.

Bad news. Her husband left her.
Good news. His clothes fit her new boyfriend.

A wise woman is one who makes her husband feel like he is master of the house, when in reality he is only part of the entertainment committee.

Blokes 'n Sheilas
Singles / Cash-and-Carried

A drinker rolled home late on a Friday night, and as he walked in, his wife was there with her hand outstretched. "O.K!" she said, "Where's your pay packet? Hand it over!" With a guilty look on his face, he pulled it out of his pocket and handed it over, saying, "You'll find it's not all there. I spent half of it on something for the house."
"Oh, that's nice. What was it?"
"A round of drinks."

****

This bloke is sitting in his favourite armchair while reading the evening paper. Suddenly his wife comes up behind him and whacks him over the head with a frying pan.
"Ouch!" he cries, "What was that for?"
"I found this note in your trouser pocket this morning. It read 'Mary Ellen' and a phone number."
"Oh, don't be silly," says the bloke. "That was the racehorse I bet on yesterday."
Next night he is reading the paper again when his wife hits him over the head with an even larger frypan.
"Hell! What have I done, now?" he asks, his head still ringing from the blow.
"Nothing," says his wife, "but your horse just phoned."

Blokes 'n Sheilas
Singles / Cash-and-Carried

They were dining out in a smart restaurant when the wife noticed a familiar face at the bar. "Thomas," she said, pointing, "do you see that man downing cognacs at the bar?" Her husband looked over and nodded.
"Well," said his wife, "he's been drinking like that for ten years now, ever since I left him."
Her husband started eating again. "Rubbish!" he said, "even that's not worth that much celebrating."

****

A woman walked into the kitchen to find her husband stalking around with a fly swatter.
"What are you doing?" she asked.
"Hunting flies," he responded.
"Oh, killing any?" she asked.
"Yep, three males and two females."
Intrigued, she asked, "How can you tell?"
"Three were on a beer can, and two were on the phone."

****

Couple in a restaurant are gazing into each other's eyes. Just as the woman glances away for a moment, the waitress comes rushing over.
"Excuse me, madam, but your husband has just slid under the table!"
"*He's* not my husband," the woman replies. "*My* husband's just walked in the door!"

****

Marriage is not a word, it's a sentence!

Blokes 'n Sheilas
Singles / Cash-and-Carried

A wealthy businessman, while on an interstate trip, calls into the local brothel and asks the receptionist for the ugliest, worst lay in the place.
The receptionist is astounded. "Sir, you obviously can afford one of our top-quality, beautiful girls. Why have you ordered the ugliest and worst girl we have?"
"Look, I'm not horny," says the businessman, "just homesick, O.K?"

****

Bloke walks into a bar and orders a double scotch. He downs it, pulls out his wallet and takes out a photo. He stares at the photo for a moment, puts it back in his wallet, and orders another double scotch.
He downs that, pulls out the photo again and examines it, before putting it away and ordering another double.
He continues this ritual for about four rounds of drinks before the barman asks him what he's up to.
"It's like this. This is a photo of the missus, and when she starts to look good, I'm goin' home."

Blokes 'n Sheilas
Singles / Cash-and-Carried

*W*hy do men die before their wives?
Because they want to.

I married Miss Right. I just didn't know her first name was Always.

*O*ur last fight was my fault. My wife asked me, "What's on the TV?" I said, "Dust."

*A*ny girl can live on love – if he's wealthy.

*W*hy don't women fart until after they get married?
They haven't got an arsehole until then.

*H*ow do men sort their laundry?
'Filthy,' and 'Filthy, but alright for another couple of days.'

*S*he finally got rid of that terrible household odour – she told her old man to get out.

*W*hat instrument does a man play once he's married?
Second fiddle.

*T*he German word for father is 'farter' – which in our house is frighteningly accurate!

Blokes 'n Sheilas
Singles / Cash-and-Carried

A woman's wedding was approaching, and she was becoming increasingly curious about sex. Matters came to a head when her parents invited her boyfriend to stay, and she blundered in on him in the bathroom. There he was, stark naked.

"Mummy," she whispered later, "what was that thing hanging down between his legs?"

"It's a penis, dear, nothing to worry about."

"And the knob on the end? Like a fireman's helmet?"

"The glans," said her mother.

"And what about the two round things about 13 inches back? What are they?"

"For your sake, dear, I hope they're the cheeks of his bum."

****

A woman who calls herself a bird deserves the worms she picks up.

A woman who thinks the way to a man's heart is through his stomach is aiming too high.

There are three kinds of men in this world – the caring, the sensitive, and the majority.

Why do men snore when they lay on their backs? Because their balls fall over their arseholes and they vapour lock!

After ecstasy – the laundry.

Blokes 'n Sheilas
Singles / Cash-and-Carried

"Marilyn," said the boastful man, "will you rate my performance on a scale of one to ten?"
"Of course, darling … may I use fractions?"

****

Two women met in the street, and one, renowned for her snide gossip, smiled sweetly.
"You poor dear," she burbled, "I know I shouldn't tell you this, but your husband has been seen running after the girl from the supermarket again."
"So let him run," the second woman shrugged. "My dog chases cars, but when he catches one, can he drive it?"

****

An elderly couple who have been married 50 years are revisiting some of the places they went on their honeymoon. As they are driving through the countryside, they see a farm bordered by a tall dingo fence.
"Let's stop," says the woman, "and do the same thing we did here fifty years ago."
The old man stops the car, backs his wife up against the fence, and they make love like a threshing machine. Exhausted, and back in the car, he says, "Darling, you were fantastic! You never moved like *that* 50 years ago!"
She says, "Fifty years ago that bloody fence wasn't electrified!"

Blokes 'n Sheilas
Singles / Cash-and-Carried

A husband comes home from work to find his wife in bed with another man. He goes absolutely bananas, ranting and raving, and calling his wife every foul name under the sun. Then he rushes to the wardrobe, pulls out his rifle, and sticks the barrel in his mouth.
His wife jumps up, screaming, "Don't do it, Bill, please!"
"Shut up, bitch!" he yells, "You're next!"

****

"Drinking makes you so handsome and desirable, sweetheart," said Joan to her husband."
"What d'you mean? I haven't touched a drop tonight."
"No," said Joan, "but I have."

****

A city bloke was driving through the country when he came across a farmer sowing his paddocks while not wearing any trousers.
"How come you're not wearing any trousers?" he asked the farmer.
"Well, mate, the other day I went out into the paddock and forgot to wear my shirt. By night time, my neck was stiffer than a board. So this is my wife's idea."

Blokes 'n Sheilas
Singles / Cash-and-Carried

Adam came first. But then, men always do.

****

A woman was in labour in hospital. As she was experiencing quite a bit of pain, the doctor said that he often asked fathers if they'd like to participate in the birthing process, and take away some of the wife's pain. The husband agreed, and the doctor got out a strange machine with a red lever. He set the lever to 10 percent, and told the husband that even 10 per cent was probably more pain than he'd ever known. However, the husband did not feel a thing. So being a macho type, he insisted that the doctor crank up the lever to 100 per cent. After it was over he stretched a little, but said that he and his wife both felt great. Later, when they took the baby home, they found the milkman dead on the doorstep.

Blokes 'n Sheilas
Singles / Cash-and-Carried

*H*er cooking is so bad, the Insinkerator has developed an ulcer!

****

*I*s my husband stupid? He's the Fred Astaire of foot-in-mouth disease.

****

*M*y wife said she bought the dress for a ridiculous figure. I said, "That's fine, but how much did you pay for it?"

*W*hy is it a good thing that there are female astronauts? At least when the crew gets lost in space, a female will ask for directions.

****

*W*oman: "Officer, officer, I've been half-raped!"
Officer: "What do you mean, you've been half-raped?"
Woman: "It was a wharfie, and it started to rain."

****

*W*hy do women rub their eyes when they get out of bed in the morning? Because they don't have balls to scratch.

Blokes 'n Sheilas
Singles / Cash-and-Carried

Two Aborigines got married and went to a motel room. He took off his trousers, and she said, "Crikey, you got small knees!"
"Yeah, I know. When I was a kid I had kneemonia, and my knees ain't grown since."
With that he took off his shoes.
"Crikey, you sure got small toes!"
"Yeah, that's 'cos when I was a kid I got toemain poisoning, and my toes ain't grown since."
Then he took off his underpants.
"Crikey, I'm glad you never got dicktheria!" said his wife.

****

Ted was tired from fishing all morning, so he went home for a nap. As it was such a lovely day his wife, Maureen, took the boat out on the lake, and sat in it reading a book. Suddenly a fisheries inspector pulled alongside and said, "You're in a restricted fishing area."
"But I'm not fishing," Maureen protested. "I'm reading a book."
"Maybe," said the inspector, "but you have all the equipment, and so I'm going to charge you."
"OK," said Maureen, "but I'm charging you with sexual assault."
"What?" snapped the inspector, "But I haven't touched you!"
"True," Maureen replied, "but you have all the equipment."

Blokes 'n Sheilas
Singles / Cash-and-Carried

"Did he go to church?" asked the undertaker.
"No," his widow replied.
"Did he belong to the Rotary?"
"No."
"Lions? Masons?"
Again the answer was no.
"Was he a member of the Klu Klux Klan?"
"What's that?" asked the widow.
"That's one of those devils under the sheets."
"Oh, he *was*," replied the widow, "most definitely he *was!*"

****

To prove his love for her, he swam the deepest river, crossed the widest desert, and climbed the highest mountain. So she divorced him, because he was never home.

A woman is sitting at a bar when a bloke sidles up to her and says, "Hi, honey, want a little company?"
"Why," she asks, "have you one to sell?"

Bushies

*B*ush *Wisdom: If you're up shit creek in a barbed wire canoe without a paddle – you're stuffed!*

A swaggie came to a small outback pub named 'George and the Dragon', and he made his way around to the back in search of a handout. Before he had time to ask, the publican's wife came on the scene and gave the swaggie the biggest tongue thrashing of his life. She called him a good-for-nothing loafer, and told him that if he was after a crust of bread, he could forget it. The swaggie heard her out in silence, and then just stood there.
"Well," she snapped, "what do you want, now?"
"I was wondering," said the swaggie, "if I could 'ave a word with George?"

The dingoes were killing the sheep on properties in a country area, and so a meeting was held in the town hall to discuss the problem. The local station owners proposed poisoning the dingoes, while the greenies were advocating castrating the dingoes as the best option.
"Bloody Hell! you bastards don't have a bloody clue, do you?" roared Dave, one of the station owners. "The dingoes are killin' the sheep, not rootin' 'em!"

Bushies

Young bloke visiting a farm for the first time sees a rooster chasing around after a hen. Just then, the farmer's wife comes out to feed them. The rooster stops chasing the hen immediately and starts eating.
"Crikey!" thinks the young bloke, "I hope I never get that hungry!"

****

Dad and Dave were at the zoo when they saw a dingo licking its privates.
"Y'know, Dad," said Dave, "I've wanted to do that all my life."
"Well, go ahead," said Dad, "but I'd pat him first. He looks pretty vicious to me."

****

Hear about the farmer who couldn't keep his hands off his wife? He sacked them all and bought a combine harvester.

****

Two boundary riders were camped for the night, and were having a smoke after their meal.
One got up to see a man about a dog, and walked into the darkness. After a minute or so, he called back to his mate, "Hey, Bill, have you ever smoked a cigarette that's been pissed on?"
Bill thought about this for a while, and then said, "No, Ted, can't say that I 'ave."
There was a silence before Ted answered, "Well, you 'aven't bloody missed much."

Bushies

A handsome man decided that it was his responsibility to marry a perfect woman in order that they could produce equally handsome children. After searching for many months, he met a farmer who had three stunningly beautiful daughters. Explaining his position to the farmer, he asked if he could marry one of them. The farmer agreed, but said that he must date each one in turn first. After dating the first daughter, the farmer asked for his opinion.
"Well," said the handsome man, "she's just a weeeeee bit – err, pigeon-toed."
The farmer nodded knowingly, and suggested he date the second daughter.
The next day, the farmer asked how that date went.
"Well," said the handsome man, "she's just a weeee bit – err, cross-eyed."
The farmer again nodded knowingly, and suggested his third daughter might be the girl of his dreams.
The next morning the handsome bloke rushed in and cried, "She's perfect, just perfect! She's the girl I want. May I have her hand in marriage?"
The farmer consented, and they were married the next day. Months later, a baby arrived. On visiting the hospital, the handsome bloke was mortified to find the baby was the ugliest, most horrible human being he had ever seen. He rushed back to the farmer and asks how such a terrible thing could happen, given the good looks of the parents.
"Ah, well," said the farmer, "she was a weeeee bit – not that you could hardly tell – err, pregnant when you proposed."

Bushies

A farmer returned from a holiday in Bali.
"Those coconuts are beaut. You can get milk out of 'em without havin' to get up at three o'clock in the mornin' and risk bein' kicked in the balls."

****

Two rabbit trappers had been around their traps and were busy gutting the rabbits. One of the trappers announced that he had to go into the bush to do a big job. His mate said, "Alright," and continued to gut, flinging the rabbits' entrails well out of the way so as to keep the work area tidy.
One set of entrails landed directly under the rabbiter as he answered the call of nature. He was gone a bit longer than usual, and when he came out of the bush his face was deathly pale, and he was barely able to walk. "Blimey, mate! What's wrong?" asked his friend.
"You wouldn't believe it," said the rabbiter, "but I strained so hard that I passed out some of me guts on to the ground." "Struth!" said his mate, "we'll have to get you to a doctor!"
"No, I'll be right," said the rabbiter." "With th' help of God and a little stick, I got 'em all back in again."

****

A bloke walked into the bar of an outback hotel.
"Long time since I've seen sawdust on the floor of a pub."
"That's not sawdust. It's yesterday's furniture after the white ants ate it."

Bushies

The old farmer was on his death bed. He beckoned to his long-suffering wife, and said, "Dearest, you were with me during the Great Depression."
His wife dabbed at a tear running down her cheek.
"You were with me during all those droughts."
She sobbed silently.
"You were with me when we lost the place in the bushfire. You were with me when the cattle prices crashed and the wool prices collapsed, and you're here when I'm about to kick the bucket."
She was openly sobbing now.
The old farmer continued: "Y' know, I'm beginnin' t' reckon you brought me nothin' but bad luck!"

****

A cowboy was out riding the range when a snake slid across his path He was just about to blow off the snake's head with his six shooter, when the snake reared up and said, "Stop! I'm a magic snake. I'll grant you three wishes if you spare my life."
The cowboy was excited. "O.K., I want to be rich, handsome, and hung like my horse."
"Done!" said the snake, and slithered away.
When the cowboy got back to the ranch, he found that the owner had died and left him everything. He then looked into the mirror and found that he was truly handsome. Nervously, he pulled down his trousers – and fainted! He had forgotten that he was riding a gelding.

Bushies

A city bloke went to the Birdsville races. After the first race, he needed to go and see a man about a dog.
Inside the toilet block he saw a long plank with ten holes in it. After nutting out how it worked, he dropped his strides and climbed aboard.
An old swaggie came in and sat on the plank, with his swag beside him, and began to roll a smoke. As he put the tobacco back into his swag, a twenty-cent piece fell out and dropped into the pit below. Without even blinking, he pulled out a twenty-dollar note and dropped it into the murky pit.
The young bloke couldn't believe his eyes, and he asked the swaggie, "What did you do that for?"
"Jeez, mate, you didn't think I was gunna dive in there fer twenty cents, did yer?"

****

The drover's wife has been on her own at the station for a few months when a swagman knocks at her door. He offers to do some chores for a few meals. Noticing that he has very big feet, the drover's wife thinks he might have a bit of potential in another department, so she welcomes him in. After a shower, a feed, and a few beers, they wind up in bed together.
When the swaggie wakes up next morning, he finds a $50 note under the pillow, with a note that reads, "Go and buy yourself a pair of shoes that fit."

****

Bush Etiquette: *If your dog falls in love with a guest's leg, have the decency to leave them alone for a few minutes.*

Bushies

"D'y know why farts smell like they do?" asked Dave.
"Guess y' gunna tell me," replied Dad.
"It's so's deaf men can enjoy them, too."

An old cocky and his son lived for many years just scratching a living from their poor farm. One day the son won $50,000 in Tattslotto. Ecstatic, he picked out a $5 note and handed it to his father.
His father looked at it for a while before saying drily, "I hope, son, that you won't go throwing your money away like this. When I was young, I never drank, smoked, gambled, or went with wild women. In fact, I never ever married."
"Well, that's great, that is!" said his son. "You know what that makes me, now, don't you?"
"Yes," replied his father, "and you're a greedy one, too!"

****

*B*ush etiquette: Although ears need to be cleaned regularly, it should be a job done in private with the ute keys.

Bushies

A young couple were driving to their honeymoon hotel when their car broke down on a country road. They made their way to the nearest farm, and asked the farmer if he could put them up for the night.

The farmer explained that they had no rooms in the house, but they were welcome to stay in the loft of the barn. There was clean hay to sleep on, and the animals wouldn't disturb them.

Three days and four nights passed, and the farmer and his wife were beginning to worry. The farmer went down to the barn, hit the wall with a spade and yelled, "Aren't you coming down to have something to eat? It's been over three days."

"It's alright," the couple called back. "We're living on the fruits of love!"

"Well," the farmer replied, "if you're livin' on the fruits of love, stop throwin' the skins out the window. They're chokin' me ducks!"

*B*ush *etiquette: Plucking unwanted nose hair is time-consuming and tedious. A cigarette lighter and a tolerance for pain can fix the trouble in half the time.*

Bushies

A farmer was down behind the chook shed repairing a wire fence as evening approached.
"Tea's ready, love!" called his wife from the back door. "You'd better come now!"
"Not yet," came the distant reply.
An hour later she called out, "You'll miss the news on telly, love. You'd better come in now."
"Not yet!"
The wife called into the darkness, "It's dark, it's late, it's getting cold. Give me three good reasons why you won't come in?"
"I'll give you four. One, I'm not hungry. Two, I don't feel like watching the telly. Three, I'm not sleepy, and four, I can't get my foot out of this bloody dingo trap!"

****

Dave took Mabel to Paris, and while she was having an afternoon nap at the hotel, he wandered off to look at the Eiffel Tower. He stood staring at it, full of wonderment and awe. There was nothing like it in Snake Gully.
After a few minutes, a pretty, young woman came up to him and whispered, "Ello, mon cher. Would you like a bit?"
"Why," asked Dave, "are they pulling it down?"

****

Cop pulls over an old farmer on a country road. "Do you realize your wife fell out of your car about twenty kilometres back?
"Well, thank God for that!" replied the farmer. "I thought I'd gone deaf!"

Bushies

A cow cocky was sitting over a beer listening to his mate, who had just returned from working in the outback....
"Then I rolled the bloody car, miles from anywhere. When I came to, I was trapped, couldn't move! D'y know, I was stuck there for two days? Not a truck, not a car, nothin' came along that bloody road!
An' then, blow me down, but two cars came along within five minutes!"
"Yeah?"
"Yeah. Was I glad t' see them – the Johnstons and the Balls."
The cow cocky thought for a moment, and then said, drily, "Hope you was dragged out by the Johnstons."

****

Tom and Dick were testing telephone lines in the outback when Tom had to answer a call of nature. Suddenly he rushed back, yelling that he had been bitten on the bum by a tiger snake.
 Dick sped up the pole, connected the wires, and was soon talking to the nearest doctor. "Hey, doc, come quickly! Me mate's been bitten on the bum by a tiger snake!"
"I can't come, now," said the doctor. "I'm in the middle of delivering a baby. Take a sharp knife, cut a nick as close to the bite as possible, and suck like Hell."
"What will happen if I don't?"
"He'll die in thirty minutes."
"What did he say?" asked Tom, when Dick had climbed down the pole.
"He said you're going to die in thirty minutes."

Bushies

This farmer who's real proud of his champion bull reckons he's on a sure thing to take out a prize at the local show.
However, a couple of days before the show, he notices the bull's gone cross-eyed. So he calls in the vet, who takes one look at the bull, pulls a rubber hose out of his bag, sticks one end in the bull's bum, and blows down the other end. The bull's eyes go back to normal.
The farmer is amazed.
"That'll be $50," says the vet, "and I'll leave you the hose, just in case."
Well, the show day comes, and the bull goes cross-eyed again.
So the farmer sticks the end of the rubber hose in the bull's bum, and blows. Nothing happens. He blows again and again. No result.
So he calls the vet again. The vet takes one look, pulls the hose out, turns it round and puts the other end back in the bull's bum, and blows hard. The bull's eyes straighten up.
"Unbelievable!" says the farmer. "Did I have the hose in the wrong way round?"
"No," says the vet, "it doesn't make any difference which way round you have it."
"Well, why did you swap ends, then?"
"Come off it, mate," says the vet, "d'y think I'd want to put that end in my mouth after you've had *your* lips around it?"

Colder than a Mother-in-law's Kiss

I never underestimate my mother-in-law – unless I'm talking about her weight or age.

*H*ear about the man who kept a portrait of his mother-in-law above the fireplace?
It kept the children away from the fire.

*M*y mother-in-law ugly? When a tear rolled down her cheek, it took one look at her face and rolled straight back up again.

*A*ttendant in the chamber of horrors: "Kindly keep your mother-in-law moving. We're stocktaking."

*M*y mother-in-law has a tongue that could slice pickles.

*M*y mother-in-law's so ugly that when she visits us, Peeping Toms knock on our door and ask us to close the curtains.

****

A golfer was having a lot of trouble with his drive. When his friend asked what the trouble was, he explained, "My mother-in-law came with me today, and she's watching me from the verandah of the clubhouse."
"Don't be a fool," said his friend. "You haven't a hope of hitting her from this distance."

Colder than a Mother-in-law's Kiss

"Look here," complained the Devil. "You've only been here a few days, and you go around as if you owned the place." "Ah, but I do," retorted the man. "My mother-in-law gave it to me while I was alive."

****

My mother-in-law makes her own yoghurt. She buys a bottle of milk and stares at it for a couple of minutes.

Doctor, my mother-in-law's dislocated her jaw. If you're passing in the next month or two, would you mind dropping in?"

Hear about the cannibal who got married and, at the reception, toasted his mother-in-law?

Colder than a Mother-in-law's Kiss

A man was told by his neighbour that his domineering mother-in-law had just died. The man remained expressionless, quite unaffected by the news.
"Your mother-in-law has died, and you show no expression at all?" asked the astonished neighbour.
"If you had a toothache like I have, you'd have trouble smiling, too," replied the man.

****

My mother-in-law is so fussy. She walked into a butcher shop one day, and grabbed hold of a dressed chicken. She picked up one wing, sniffed it; picked up the other wing, sniffed it; picked up one leg, sniffed it; picked up the other leg, sniffed it. The butcher could contain himself no longer. He walked over to her and said, "Madam, could *you* pass such a test?"

****

My mother-in-law thinks I'm effeminate. Compared to her, I probably am!

The penalty for bigamy is having two mothers-in-law.

My mother-in-law is so mean that when she takes a dollar out of her purse, Queen Elizabeth blinks at the light.

Ugly? They used my mother-in-law's photo in prison to cure sex offenders.

Colder than a Mother-in-law's Kiss

They now have a mother-in-law's sandwich – cold shoulder with salty tongue.

I'd like to smother my mother-in-law in diamonds – but there must be a cheaper way.

Adam was the luckiest man in the world – no mother-in-law. That's how we know he lived in Paradise.

Think you've got troubles? My mother-in-law has a twin sister.

They ran some tests on my mother-in-law for PMT. It turns out she never actually had it – she's ALWAYS been a bitch.

I've just got back from a pleasure trip – took my mother-in-law to the station.

A mother's Wedding Telegram to her daughter. 'Twenty-three years ago I sent you to bed with a dummy. Tonight history repeats itself.'

I had my mother-in-law cremated AND buried – I wasn't taking any chances!

Flesh-pressers

You can always tell when a politician lies. His lips are moving.

What's the difference between a dead dog in the road, and a dead politician in the road?
Skid marks in front of the dog.

There are things all political parties have in common – our money.

Two things I don't like about our local member – his face!

Sign in men's toilet over hot air blower for drying hands:
PRESS BUTTON TO HEAR SHORT MESSAGE FROM THE PRIME MINISTER

A sign outside the Free Range Lion Wildlife Park:
ADULTS, $10 CHILDREN, $5 POLITICIANS, *FREE*

Politicians will find an excuse to get out of anything – except office.

Nappies and politicians should be changed frequently – and just as often.

A politician – about as popular as a piranha in a bidet.

Flesh-pressers

She was Conservative while he was Labor, but they decided to live together on the basis of agreeing to disagree. One night a television programme set off the traditional argument. When they went to bed, she remained on the Right, he on the Left.

Eventually she whispered, "There is a split in the Tories, and it is likely that if the Labor member stood, he could slip in unopposed."

"Too late," he said, "There's been too much stimulation in the private sector, and he has blown his deposit."

****

A scientist, a salesman and a politician are travelling together through the countryside, and decide to spend the night at a small pub. "I only have two spare beds, so one of you will have to sleep in the barn," says the hotelier. The scientist volunteers to do so, and makes his way out to the barn. However, a short time later, he returns. "There's a cow in the barn. I'm Hindu, and it's against my religion to sleep with a sacred animal." So the salesman says, "O.K, I'll sleep out there, then." He gathers up his blankets and goes outside, but returns a little later. "There's a pig in the barn. I'm Jewish, and it's against my religion to sleep next to an unclean animal." So the politician is sent to the barn. A minute later, there is a loud knocking on the door. When the scientist and salesman open the door, they see the cow and the pig standing there.

Flesh-pressers

The cocky went into town and bought a colour telly. He took it home in the back of his ute, and tried it out. Then he rang the television store, spewing.

"This bloody telly you sold me. All I get on it is politicians. No matter what channel I turn to, it's only bloody politicians!"

The store said they'd send a repair man out. When he got back to town, the shop owner asked the repair man what had happened.

"The poor bloke really did have a problem," said the repair man. "Nothing but politicians on every channel. You see, he was using his windmill for an antenna, and had the thing earthed to his manure spreader!"

The Premier was having great difficulty getting any good press coverage. So he arranged for all the press to gather under the Sydney Harbour bridge next day for an important announcement.

When they were all assembled, the Premier thought, "I'm going to do something no-one can complain about." He then proceeded to walk on the water across Sydney Harbour.

Next day the headlines in the Herald read, 'PREMIER CAN'T SWIM', while the Telegraph stated, 'GOVERNMENT RORTS. PREMIER DOESN'T PAY TOLL!'

Flesh-pressers

Did you hear about the politician who proclaimed he was a self-made man?
At least he was willing to take the blame.

****

A politician was driving a constituent and her son through Kings Cross when the boy pointed to some women loitering on the footpath. "What are those ladies waiting for?" he asked.
His mother replied, "They are waiting for their husbands to pick them up from work."
The politician cut in, "Lady, you can't shield your son from the real world. Why don't you admit to him that they're prostitutes?"
The boy then asked, "Do prostitutes have babies?"
His mother replied, "Of course, dear. Where do you think politicians come from?"

****

The polls are places where you stand in line for a chance to decide who will spend your money.

****

A politician who says he will stick to the facts has no respect for tradition.

The only time the politician got a standing ovation was when he addressed the Australian Haemorrhoid Association.

Funny Buggers, All of Us

A friend is one who knows all about you – and likes you regardless.

A big, bronzed Aussie was up before the beak for pinching a lady's bike. When the beak asked him how he pleaded, he said, "Not guilty, yer honour. Y'see, I was sittin' on a seat in the park when this wog sheila rode up, got off 'er bike, an' sat next t' me. We 'ad a bit of a yarn, an' the next thing she grabbed me an' said, "Oh, you da beeg, brown Australian. You can have a whatever you want." So I took the bike."

****

An Englishman, a German, a Scotsman and an Irishman are sitting around the canteen discussing how stupid their wives are. The Englishman says, "My wife is so stupid that last week she bought $400 worth of meat on special, and we don't even own a freezer!"
"That's nothing!" says the German, "My wife bought $2,000 worth of ski equipment, and she can't even ski!"
"I can top that," says the Scotsman. "Last week my wife bought a $45,000 sports car, and she's never driven in her life!"
The Irishman starts laughing. "Beat this! My wife is so stupid, on her last visit to Greece, I watched her put at least 200 condoms in her bag, and she hasn't even got a penis!"

****

Eloquence of the Australian male: Better conversations in an alphabet soup.

Funny Buggers, All of Us

Four blokes were travelling in this car. One was a Tasmanian, one was a South Aussie, and there was a Queenslander, and a Victorian. Suddenly the Tasmanian opened his window and threw out a bag of apples.
"Why did you do that?" asked the others.
"Oh," said the Tasmanian, "I'm sick of the sight of apples. Everywhere I go in Tassie, it's apples, apples, apples."
A little later, the South Aussie opened his window, and threw out a couple of bottles of wine.
"What's that all about?" asked the others.
"Oh," said the South Aussie, "Everywhere I go in South Australia, there's nothing but wine."
With that the Queenslander opened his window, and threw out the Victorian.

****

When Abe Goldstein came home from the shop his wife told him that she had just bought a block of flats in their name.
He was delighted, and they celebrated with a few drinks. As he was thinking about the situation he said, "Miriam, where did you get the money from to buy a block of flats?"
She explained that during their thirty years of marriage, whenever they made love, she had deposited $10 in a special account at the bank.
"Miriam, you foolish girl," said Abe, "Why didn't you tell me? I could have given you ALL my business!"

Average Aussie watches 20 hours of television a week – slightly more when it's turned on.

Funny Buggers, All of Us

A tourist arrives at an outback Australian pub. He orders a meal and a glass of water. After a while, the meal arrives, but not the water.
"What do you do to get a glass of water in this dump?" he asks.
The cook replies, "Well, you could try settin' fire t' yerself!"

****

Maureen's husband, Mick, worked night shift at the local distillery. She was surprised one evening when a policeman knocked on her door.
"I'm sorry to inform you, Madam," he said, "but your husband has had an accident."
"Oh, my God, what happened, and how is he?"
"I'm afraid to tell you that he fell into a vat of whisky and has died."
"Tell me, officer, did he suffer much?"
"We don't think so, Madam," said the policeman. "He got out six times to go to the toilet."

Heard about the Aussie who thought that a penal colony was an all-male nudist camp?

Funny Buggers, All of Us

An Englishman, an American and an Irishman were discussing world history, and one of them posed a question, "Which do you think is the most significant invention of the century?"

The Englishman thought it was the telephone. "You can speak to someone anywhere in the world in a matter of seconds."

The American was convinced that it must be the aeroplane. "You can fly anywhere in the world in a matter of hours."

The Irishman thought it must be the thermos flask he had on the table.

"You must be kidding," said the American. "That only keeps things hot or cold."

"Yes," said the Irishman, "but how does it know?"

****

Why do Aussie men come quickly?
So's they can get to the pub, and tell their mates about it.

****

"I'll give this shiny apple to anyone who can tell me who was the greatest man in the world," said the teacher.

David Epstein shot his hand up, "It was Jesus, miss."

"Well done," said the teacher, "but I thought you were Jewish."

David said, "Yes, miss, I am – and *YOU* know and *I* know that Moses was the greatest man in the world, but business is business."

Funny Buggers, All of Us

An American firm drilling for oil in northern Australia employed a few Aussies as labourers. One of the Australians accidentally dropped a heavy hammer down the shaft. Further drilling was impossible until it was removed, and much time and money was spent in retrieving it. Then the manager assembled the men around the shaft, and presented the Aussie with the offending hammer.

"I want you to accept this hammer as a memento of the trouble you've caused," he said sarcastically. "Now take it and GO!"

"Does that mean I'm sacked?" asked the Aussie.

"It sure does!"

"Well, then, this thing is no flamin' use t' me," said the Aussie, and dropped it neatly down the shaft again.

****

A posh Australian woman, and a down-to-earth Italian woman were in a maternity ward after the delivery of their children.

"When my first child was born," said the posh Australian, "my husband gave me a mink coat."

"That's-a-nice," replied the Italian lady.

"And when my second child was born," the first lady went on, "he gave me a new Mercedes."

"That's-a-nice."

"And tell me," said the posh Australian, "what did your husband give you for your first baby?"

"He give-a me a book on etiquette," said the Italian lady.

"Why a book on etiquette?"

"Well, I used to say-a BULLSHIT, but now I just-a say, 'THAT'S-A-NICE.'"

Funny Buggers, All of Us

An Aussie was having coffee and croissants with butter and jam in a café when an American tourist, chewing gum, sat down beside him.

The American immediately started up a conversation. He snapped the gum in his mouth and asked, "Do you Australian folk eat the whole bread?"

The Aussie frowned, annoyed with being bothered during his breakfast and replied, "Yeah, of course."

The American blew a huge bubble, and smirked, "We don't. In the States we only eat what's inside. The crusts we collect in a container, recycle them into croissants, and sell them to Australia."

He persisted, "D'ya eat jam with the bread?"

Sighing, the Aussie replied, "Yeah."

Cracking his gum between his teeth, the American went on, "We don't. In the States we eat fresh fruit for breakfast, put all the peel, seeds and leftovers in containers, recycle it into jam, and sell it to Australia."

The Aussie then asked, "D'y have sex in the States?"

The American smiled, "Of course we do."

The Aussie then leant closer to him and asked, "What d'y do with the condoms once you've used them?"

"We throw them away, of course," replied the American.

"We don't," smiled the Aussie. "In Australia we put them in containers, recycle them, melt them into chewing gum, and sell it to the United States. That's why it's branded Wrigleys."

****

*S*he said she would never go to a restaurant with Jock McTavish again. *"He reads the menu from right to left."*

Funny Buggers, All of Us

During World War One, Australian troops who were badly wounded were repatriated to England for medical treatment. After being discharged from hospital, Private Smith found he had to wait three hours for the next train, and so he took himself to the railway bar.
After three hours drinking he was in a tired and emotional state when the call for his train came through.
The carriage was First Class and as such, was available to officers only, and so he knew he was in trouble when he sat down between two colonels.
Casting a black look in the Aussie's direction, one officer said to the other, "Allow me to introduce myself. I'm Colonel Llewellyn-Jones, British Army, educated Oxford, married, one son, a doctor."
The other officer responded, "I am Colonel Forsythe, British Army, educated Cambridge, married, one son, a lawyer."
There was silence for a while, and then the Aussie spoke up, "Private Smith, Australian Army, educated Bullamakanka State School, single, two sons, both Colonels in the British Army."

****

Hear about the Irishman who refused to buy a pocket calculator?"
He already knew how many pockets he had.

****

"What would ye be chargin'," asked Murphy, "to put me brother's death notice in the paper?"
"50p an inch."
"Glory be! – an' me brother was six feet tall!"

Funny Buggers, All of Us

In Australia it is considered better to be down on your luck than up yourself.

****

An Aberdeen pub offers free drinks to pensioners, provided they are accompanied by their parents.

****

A reporter in Jerusalem has an apartment overlooking the Western Wall. Every day she sees the same old Jew there, praying energetically. Thinking there might be a story there, she approaches the old man and asks, "How long have you been coming to the wall to pray, and what do you pray for?"
"I've come here to pray for 25 years. In the morning I pray for world peace. Then I pray for the brotherhood of man. Then I go home for a small lunch, and return to pray for the eradication of illness and disease. In the late afternoon, I pray for an end to ant-Semitism and other forms of bigotry."
"And how does it make you feel to come and pray every day for 25 years for such worthy causes?"
And the old man says, "Like I'm talking to a wall."

****

How do you recognize a Bondi lifesaver?
They're the ones who pull their Speedos up their cracks to keep the left and right sides of their brains separate.

Funny Buggers, All of Us

An Irishman working in an Arab country where alcohol was banned was stopped at the customs counter after returning from a holiday in France.
"What's in this bottle?" asked the customs officer, taking out a large bottle from the Irishman's bag.
"Tis Holy Water from Lourdes."
The customs officer opened the bottle and sniffed suspiciously, and then tasted a little of it. "Hmmm, it looks, smells and tastes like whisky to me, sir."
"Glory be!" exclaimed the Irishman, "'tis another miracle!"

****

An Englishman, a Scotsman and an Australian were flying over New Guinea when their plane crash-landed in the jungle. They were captured by cannibals, taken to the village and paraded, one by one, before the Chief.
The Englishman was the first to be ushered in, and he asked what his fate was to be. "We will skin you alive, eat you, and make a canoe out of your skin," said the Chief.
The Englishman immediately begged for a knife so that he could end this torture by taking his own life. His wish was granted.
The Scotsman was then brought before the Chief and, being told of his fate, begged for a knife to end his own life. His wish was granted.
When the Australian was told of his fate, he considered a moment, and then asked for a fork. The Chief was bewildered, but granted his request. The Australian took the fork in his hand, stabbed himself in the stomach and chest and shouted, "You'll never make a canoe out of me!"

Funny Buggers, All of Us

An American was touring around Australia, and was not at all impressed. One night, in a bar in Darwin, he began telling the locals exactly what he thought of their country. He complained that the beer was too cold, the food was stodgy, the shops closed too early, the roads were bad, the trains were late, the TV programmes were awful, the men were boring and uncouth, and the women were ugly.
"In fact, this whole goddam country is the arsehole of the world!"
"Oh," the barman shrugged, "just passing through, are you?"

****

An Aussie bloke was showing an American visitor around Sydney. When they came to the GPO the American asked how long it took to build it.
"Oh," said the Aussie, "about twelve months."
"That would only take us six months in the States," said the American.
Then they came to another large building.
"How long did it take to build this?" the American asked.
"About three months," answered the Aussie, thinking that this would stump the American.
"In the States, that would only take six weeks."
When they came to the Sydney Harbour Bridge, the American asked, "How long did it take to build *that*, Aussie?"
The Aussie thought for a moment and scratched his head. "Gee, mate, it wasn't there yesterday!"

Funny Buggers, All of Us

Ad in Irish paper:
FOR SALE
Secondhand tombstone. Excellent buy for someone named Murphy.

****

Kelly returned from his first holiday abroad, and he didn't look too happy. "Did you enjoy yourself?" asked his neighbour.
"Well, t' tell y' t' truth, I'm so glad I'm home, I'm not sorry I went."

****

An Aborigine went into an enormous pig farm looking for work. The foreman smirked to himself, and told him he had just the job for him. All he had to do was arrive at 5 a.m., and load a truckload of pigs by 9 a.m. The foreman knew that it took a couple of experienced blokes all day to get the pigs on board.
Next day the Aborigine turned up at 5, and at 6 o'clock he bowled up to the foreman and told him that he had finished.
"Pull the other leg," said the disbelieving foreman.
But it was true. The truck was loaded with pigs.
"How the hell did you do that?" asked the foreman. "It must have been beginner's luck."
The Aborigine smiled and said nothing.
The next two days the same thing happened. The Aborigine got the job done in a fraction of the time. The foreman decided to hide in the bushes the next day.
The Aborigine let the pigs out of the yard, stood in the back of the truck and sang, "Come on, Aussie, come on!"

Funny Buggers, All of Us

Mick is in court being charged with causing an affray. He looks very much the worse for wear with cuts and bruises. The other person involved in the brawl is Sean.
"Tell me what happened, Mick," asks the judge.
"Well, your honour, I was in the bar mindin' me own business when Sean came in with a long piece of four-be-two in his hand, and began beatin' me. Oi didn't stand a chance. Oi definitely was the innocent party."
"But Mick, what did you have in your hand?" asks the judge.
"Ah, your honour, all I had in my hand was Molly Maguire's right breast. 'Twas a lovely ting, t' be sure, but no earthly good in a fight!"

****

A Pommy got a job on a cattle station. He mucked up every job he was given to do.
Finally the farmer gave him his last chance. He told the Pommy to take the heifer into the paddock with the Hereford bull. Later the farmer asked him how it had gone.
"Top hole, old chap," said the Pom.
"Jesus Christ, you stuffed it up again!" said the farmer.

****

Moses went back up the mountain. "Listen, God, I just want to get this straight. The Arabs get all the oil, and we have to cut the ends off our what?????????"

Funny Buggers, All of Us

A Chinaman had a fruit and vegie shop in a very multicultural part of Melbourne. Each Friday, his Greek neighbour from the snack bar next door used to pass his shop on the way to bank his takings, and he would call out, "What day is it, Chinaman?"
The Chinaman always replied, "Flyday, you Gleek plick."
"Not 'Flyday', you little bastard, Fr-r-r-riday. Why don't you learn to speak English proper?"
So the Chinaman practised all week. Next Friday when the Greek called out, "What day is it, Chinaman?" he answered, "Fr-r-r-riday, you Gleek plick."

****

During World War II the train from Leeds to London was absolutely full, and many soldiers had been wearily standing in the corridors for hours. A wealthy woman, ignoring their plight, had been occupying two seats, one for herself, and one for her poodle, in the first class compartment. An English officer politely asked her if she would mind putting her dog on the floor.
"I have paid for this seat, and Fifi can stay there as long as she wants," she said disdainfully.
Eventually the officer could stand it no longer. He picked up the poodle, threw it out of the window, and sat down. There was stunned silence for a moment before an American officer sitting opposite, leaned over towards the English officer, and said, "You English are a funny lot. You eat with your fork in the wrong hand, drive on the wrong side of the road, and now you've thrown the wrong bitch out the window!"

Funny Buggers, All of Us

The shearers had been giving the Chinese cook buggery. They'd put snails in his boots, spiders under his pillow, and a dead snake in his coat pocket. Finally they felt a bit sorry for the poor bloke, and said that they wouldn't do it any more.
"No more spiders?" asked the cook.
"No," they promised.
"No more snakes? No more snails?"
"No, no more tricks," they said.
"Okay, then I stop pissing in soup."

****

A digger during the last war was posted to a remote part of the Western Desert. One day he received a letter from his mother. "John, it is wonderful to get your letters, but we've almost forgotten what you look like. Could you send us a photo?" Although there was a shortage of photographers in the Western Desert, he did have a photo of himself that a mate had taken. Trouble was that he was starkers, except for his slouch hat. So he cut the photo in half, and sent his Mum the top bit.
The next letter from his mother read, "Thank you, darling, for the marvellous photo, but could you also send one to Granny? She's always asking after you."
He only had the bottom half of the photo, but he thought that as Granny was practically blind, she wouldn't be able to see the details. So he sent Granny the bottom half.
In due course he got a reply from Granny.
"Dear John. How wonderful of you to send me a photograph. You know, you're getting more like your father all the time. You have bags under your eyes. You need a shave. And what's more, your tie isn't straight."

God-botherers

A definition of a masochist:- a celibate priest, because he gives up his sex life only to have people come in and tell him the highlights.

A young, married minister went to his congregation, informed them of his wife's pregnancy, and asked for a raise in salary in order to cope with his new circumstances. After much deliberation it was agreed that the increase in family size warranted an increase in salary.
After six births in six years, the congregation thought that the cost was becoming burdensome, and called a meeting. The meeting became rather heated, until finally the minister stood at the altar and shouted, "Having children is an act of God!"
"Snow and rain are acts of God, too," shouted a man at the back of the church, "but most of us wear rubbers!"

****

Two missionaries in Africa were captured by a tribe of hostile cannibals who put them in a large pot of water, built a fire under it, and left them there. As the water boiled and the heat grew more intense, one of the missionaries began to laugh hysterically.
The other missionary couldn't believe it! He said, "What's wrong with you? We're being cooked alive! They're going to eat us! What could possibly be funny at a time like this?" The other missionary said with a gleeful smile, "I just pissed in the soup!"

God-botherers

The priest was about to be transferred to Rome, so before he departed his village, he offered to light a candle at the Vatican for the Kellys, a couple who had been childless for six years.
Ten years later, the priest returned to the village to find that the Kellys had nine children in the family. Congratulating Mrs Kelly, he asked where her husband was.
"Oh, him," replied the poor haggard woman, "he's gone to Rome to blow out the candle."

****

A rabbi was horrified when a young businessman called Moses 'a fool.'
"How dare you!" thundered the rabbi, "What possible reason could you have for saying such a thing?"
"Well." shrugged the young man, "if he had turned right instead of left, *We'd* own the oil wells!"

****

A young nun goes to confession and tells the priest she has a terrible secret.
"That's alright," says the priest. "Whatever you say in the confessional is confidential. What is your secret?"
"I never wear any panties under my habit, Father," says the nun.
"That's not so serious," smiles the priest to himself. "Say five Hail Marys, five Our Fathers, and do six cartwheels on your way to the altar!"

God-botherers

As the proud father handed the baby to the vicar at the christening font, the cleric asked, "And what do we call this little chap?"
"It's a girl," whispered the father. "You've got hold of my thumb!"

****

St Peter was checking in the new arrivals at the Pearly Gates.
"Name?" he said.
"Lulu Bell," she replied.
"Cause of death?"
"The clap," she said.
"Couldn't be," said St Peter. "No-one dies of the clap."
"You do when you give it to Big John."

****

A nun was a few miles from her convent one day when her car ran out of petrol. Luckily, a passing motorist stopped to see if he could help.
"I just need some petrol," said the nun.
"Well, I can give you some petrol, but I don't have anything to put it in," said the motorist.
Remembering that she had a bedpan in the boot of the car, the nun gave it to him, and in no time the man had siphoned some petrol from his tank into the bedpan. As she began to fill her tank from the bedpan, he drove off. Just then another motorist drove by. Seeing what the nun was doing, he said to his passenger, "Now that's what I call faith."

God-botherers

A priest and a minister were sitting next to each other while travelling on a plane. The hostess asked the priest if he would like a drink. He replied, "Scotch and soda, please."
She then asked the minister if he'd like the same. "No, thanks," he replied, "I'd rather commit adultery than consume alcohol."
The priest turned to the hostess and said, "May I change my order? I didn't know I had a choice."

****

The vicar asked the young lad, "Who went to Mount Olive?"
"Popeye," was the quick reply.

****

A naïve young Sydney priest had to walk back from his rounds through Kings Cross. A lady of the night approached him and asked, "$200 for a naughty, Father?" Not knowing what to make of this, he continued on his way. The same thing happened several more times, each girl asking for the same amount. Eventually he arrived back at the seminary, where he asked Mother Superior, "Mother, what's a naughty?"
"Look, it's $200 – the same as up the Cross. Take it or leave it!"

****

The priest admonished the villagers, "You must not use the pill."
The young signorina replied, "You no play the game, you no make the rules."

God-botherers

A minister at a small country church proposed to direct his next sermon to the young people. After thinking about it, he decided to make his subject water skiing. His wife thought that he didn't know enough about the subject, and tried to discourage him. In fact, she decided to stay at home rather than see him make a fool of himself.

As he walked to church, the minister thought that perhaps his wife was right, and decided to make sex his subject, as they all seemed to be interested in that.

Next day the church organist met the wife in town and told her that it was a pity that she wasn't in church as the minister had given a wonderful sermon to the young people. "I didn't want to see him talking on something he knows absolutely nothing about," said the wife. "He's only tried it twice. Once before we were married, and once after, and he fell off both times."

****

Every year in a little country town the kids from the Catholic school competed against the kids from the State school in a sports carnival, which was followed by a party. One year the State school won every event, which did not go down well with the local priest who was presiding over the party. Desperately anxious to score a point somewhere, he noticed that four of the State school kids were missing, and he sent one of the nuns to find them. "Any luck, Sister?" he asked when she returned. "Yes, Father, I found them. They were in the toilet, seeing who could pee the highest up the wall."

"Goodness me! So what did you do?" asked the priest. "Naturally, Father," said the nun, "I hit the roof."

"Praise the Lord!" cried the priest, "We finally beat them at something!"

God-botherers

*Why wasn't Christ born in Australia?
Because He couldn't find a virgin or Three Wise Men.*

The mother superior was giving her graduating class a few words of advice before they left the convent. "You are about to go out into the sinful world. I must warn you against some men who will whisper rude suggestions to you, buy you drinks, take you to their rooms, undress you and offer you money to do rude things."
"Excuse me, Mother," said an attractive young girl, "did you say these wicked men would give us money?"
"Yes, child, why do you ask?"
"Father O'Malley only gives us lollies."

****

An elderly couple were watching a TV evangelist. He said that he was going to transmit some spiritual healing through the telly, and he asked the viewers to put one hand on their hearts and the other on the organ which needed healing.
The old lady put one hand on her heart, and one on her arthritic hip.
The old man had one hand on his heart, and the other on his genitals.
"Heavens sake, Tom," said the old woman, "he aims to heal the sick, not raise the dead!"

*What do you get when you cross a Jehovah's witness with a bikie?
Someone who knocks on your door and tells YOU to piss off!*

Limerick Lulus / Bush Wisdom

Said a printer well known for his wit,
"There are certain bad words we omit.
It would sully our art
To print the word f...
And we never, no never, use sh..."

****

We once had two dunnies outside,
But Mother fell down one and died,
My uncle, her brother,
Then fell down the other,
And now they're interred side by side.

A plumber one night feeling free
Was plumbing his girl by the sea.
Said the maid, "Quick, stop plumbing,
I fear someone's coming."
Said the plumber, still plumbing, "It's me!"

Limerick Lulus / Bush Wisdom

There was a town tart, lived in Sale,
With prices tattooed on her tail,
For the sake of the blind,
There on her behind
It was even written in braille.

****

At a wedding reception in Bright
The groom drank for half of the night,
His intoxication
Meant no consummation,
'Cause the groom, not the bride was too tight.

In the harem a lonely girl calls,
But the guard takes no notice at all.
When asked if he cheats
On the sultan, he bleats,
"Oh, I would, but I ain't got the balls."

Limerick Lulus / Bush Wisdom

***B**USH WISDOM:*

The wind blew so hard it took the pricks off a barbed wire fence.

A dashing young dentist, Malone
Attends all the nice women alone,
And tries, from depravity,
To fill every cavity,
It's the reason his practice has grown.

****

Though I've studied me Bible real good,
There's one thing that I've not understood:
It's why Noah, the clot,
Didn't up with his swat
And kill both them flies while he could!

****

A renegade priest from Liberia,
Whose morals were clearly inferior,
Once did to a nun
What he shouldn't have done,
And now she's a Mother Superior.

****

***B**USH WISDOM:*

Remember, even a kick up the bum is a step forward.

Limerick Lulus / Bush Wisdom

"Your car's in a 'NO STANDING' street,
"So you're booked," said the cop on the beat.
Said the driver, "Fair go!
We weren't standin' y'know –
We was stretched out across the back seat!"

****

At the beach there are surfies and rockers,
And the girls who leave tops in their lockers.
Some are short, some are tall,
Some boobs large, some boobs small,
You could say we're a nation of knockers!

"And what'll y'ave?" said the waiter,
Idly picking his nose.
Thinks, 'He's really the dregs.'
"I'll have two hard-boiled eggs,
You can't put your finger in THOSE!"

Limerick Lulus / Bush Wisdom

There was a young actor named Bates,
Who danced the fandango on skates,
But he fell on his cutlass
Which rendered him nutless,
And practically useless on dates.

There is a young lady named Aird,
Whose bottom is always kept bared;
When asked why, she pouts,
And says the Boy Scouts
All beg her to Please Be Prepared.

****

An old archeologist named Tossel
Discovered a marvellous fossil.
He knew from its bend
And the knob on the end,
'Twas the peter of Paul the Apostle.

****

BUSH WISDOM:
The best way to make a bull sweat is to give him a tight jersey.

Limerick Lulus / Bush Wisdom

He sat next to the duchess at tea.
It was just as he feared it would be.
Her rumblings abdominal
Were just astronomical,
And everyone thought it was he.

There was a young man from Australia,
Who painted his arse like a dahlia.
The drawing was fine,
The colour divine,
But the scent? Ar, that was a failure.

****

There was a Scot named McIvers,
His knackers were two different sizes.
One was so small
It was no ball at all,
But the other won several first prizes.

****

BUSH WISDOM: *A farm is a hunk of land on which, if you get up early in the morning, and work late enough, you'll make a fortune – if you strike oil.*

Limerick Lulus / Bush Wisdom

A redheaded swagman from Cooee
Wed a maiden with eyes big and dewy.
The bride was elated
As she anticipated
The pleasure of humping her bluey.

****

A history teacher from Young
Was fired for a slip of her tongue –
She told a young minion
That, in her opinion,
Ned Kelly was very well hung.

****

A pregnant myopic from Drouin
Blamed glasses for causing her ruin,
"When boys wanted sex
They'd breathe on my specs
So I couldn't see what I was doin'."

****

A lass from the Diamantina
Found fame in the showbiz arena.
Her talents though few,
(in fact, only two),
Were enormous, said those who had seen 'er.

Limerick Lulus / Bush Wisdom

A guide at the Rock, Uluru,
Was vexed by a stone in his shoe.
He wasn't a wimp,
But the pain made him limp,
So his girlfriend was vexed by it, too.

****

There was a young stud called Sir Lancelot,
Whom his neighbours would glance at askance a lot.
For whenever he'd pass
A presentable arse,
The front of his pants would advance a lot.

****

At Gosford, beside Brisbane Water,
A swimming coach lectured his daughter,
"You can teach the young blokes
All the overarm strokes,
But the breaststroke, I don't think you oughta."

****

A stockman from Kangaroo Flat
Was aroused by his boss's wife, Pat.
Too shy to confess,
He concealed his distress
By keeping it under his hat.

BUSH WISDOM:
To get rid of a boomerang, throw it down a one-way street.

Medico Mirth

A doctor is the only man who can tell a woman to take off all her clothes, and then send her husband a bill for it.

A man rushed into the doctor's surgery in a very agitated state.
"I must see the doctor quickly. There's something wrong with my willy!"
The receptionist was shocked. "You can't come in here saying things like that in front of the other people in the waiting room. I suggest you go out and come in again, and say you have something wrong with your...er...ear."
The man did as he was told and came in again. "I have something wrong with my ear."
"Oh," said the receptionist, "and what is wrong with your ear?"
"I can't piss out of it."

****

A woman with twelve kids arrived at the doctor's surgery, and said, "Doctor, I have some good news. I'll never be pregnant again, thanks to my new instrument."
"What is this instrument?" asked the doctor, puzzled.
"It's my hearing aid," she replied. "Now I can hear properly."
"How does that help?" asked the doctor.
"Before I had this, my husband would say, "Shall we go straight to sleep or what?" and I'd say, 'what?'"

****

What's the use of consulting your doctor about a cold if it gives you heart disease when you get the bill?

Medico Mirth

A sea captain arrived home after 18 months at sea to discover that his wife was pregnant.
"How can this be?" he asked the doctor.
"It's what we call 'revenge pregnancy,' the doctor explained.
"I don't understand," said the sailor.
"It means someone's had it in for you," the doctor explained.

****

During a medical conference, two of the doctors became attracted to each other, and it wasn't long before they went up to her hotel room.
"Excuse me a moment," she said, "I've just got to wash my hands, and then I'll pour us a drink." After a couple of gin and tonics they went to the bedroom, and again she excused herself while she washed her hands. After their moments of passion, she again went and washed her hands. After she returned, the male doctor said, "I bet you're a surgeon."
"Yes," she said, surprised, "how did you guess?"
"Because you're always washing your hands."
"And I bet you're an anaesthetist," she said.
"How did you guess?" he asked.
"Well, I didn't feel a thing," she said.

****

He told the doctor that he's never get circumcised because he'd have no place to put his chewing gum. (Ugh!)

Medico Mirth

As the old couple entered his surgery, the doctor asked, "What can I do for you?"
"We'd like you to watch us making love," said the man.
The doctor was quite puzzled, but agreed, and when they had finished, he said, "There's nothing wrong with the way you make love," and charged them eighteen dollars for the consultation.
This happened several weeks in a row. They would make an appointment, make love, pay the doctor his eighteen dollars, and leave. Finally the doctor asked, "What exactly are you trying to find out?"
"We're not trying to find out anything," said the old man. "She's married, so we can't go to her house, and I'm married, so we can't go to mine. The Hilton Hotel will charge us a hundred dollars, the Motel will charge us sixty-five, so we come here for eighteen dollars, and get twelve back from Medicare."

****

While acquainting himself with a new elderly patient, the doctor asked, "How long have you been bedridden?"
After a look of confusion the old lady answered, "Not for about twenty years, when my husband was alive."

****

When I told my doctor about my loss of memory, he made me pay in advance.

****

"Oh, doctor," she said coyly, "where will I put my clothes?"
"Put them over there, next to mine."

Medico Mirth

A few days before a proctological (rear end) examination, a one-eyed patient accidentally swallows his glass eye. He rings his GP who tells him not to worry, and that nature will take its course in due time.
At the proctologist's office, the patient undresses and bends over. Of course, the first thing the specialist sees when he looks up is the glass eye staring back at him.
"You know, Mr Jones," says the specialist, "you're really going to have to learn to trust me."

****

A man limped into the doctor's surgery.
"What seems to be the trouble?" the doctor asked.
"I reckon it's housemaid's knee, doctor."
"What makes you think that?"
"My wife caught her sitting on it," replied the man.

****

She told the doctor that every time she sneezed she had an orgasm.
"What have you been taking for it?" asked the doctor.
"Pepper," she replied.

Medico Mirth

Two doctors were sitting on a park bench when they noticed an old man approaching. His knees were pressed together, and his fists were tightly clenched and bent inwards.
One doctor nudged the other. "You still think you can diagnose on sight. Have a go at this bloke."
"Arthritis. No doubt about it."
"No, I'd bet on cerebral palsy," said the other doctor.
They were about to ask the old man, when he shuffled up to them and said through clenched teeth, "Excuse me, d'you know where the shithouse is?"

****

An old couple told the doctor at the fertility clinic that they would like another baby.
"Well," said the doctor, "it might not be easy at your age. We'll need a sperm sample to begin with."
The couple were handed a jar, and directed to a nearby cubicle.
Grunts and groans came from the cubicle, but it was nearly three hours before they appeared, both red in the face from their exertions.
"Everything alright?" asked the doctor. "Not really," said the old man. "First I used my right hand, then my left hand, and my wife tried, too, but we still can't unscrew the lid of the jar."

****

My doctor tells me I've got too much blood in my alcohol system.

Medico Mirth

The doctor was perplexed as he studied the patient's test report.
"It appears that your test results are mixed up with those of another patient. Either you've got Alzheimer's disease or AIDS."
"That's terrible," said the patient. "What shall I do?"
"All I can suggest," said the doctor, "is that if you can find your way home, that you don't have sex with your wife."

****

A trade union leader went to his doctor for help in getting to sleep. The doctor was reluctant to put him on to sleeping pills until other remedies had been tried first.
He asked the man to lie quite still in bed at night, and count sheep jumping fences.
The trade union leader did this, but by the time he'd counted the twenty-seventh sheep, they'd all gone on strike for shorter hours and lower fences.

A man wakes up in hospital after a horrific motor accident.
"Doctor, help me, I can't feel my legs."
"Not surprising," says the doctor, "I had to amputate your arms."

Medico Mirth

The doctor had just finished examining a very attractive girl.

"Have you been going out with men, Miss Rush?"

"Oh, no, doctor, never!"

"Are you quite sure, bearing in mind that I have now examined the sample you sent? Do you still say you've never had anything to do with men?"

"Quite sure, doctor. Can I go now?"

"No," said the doctor.

"Why not?" asked Miss Rush.

"Because, Miss Rush, I'm waiting for the arrival of the Three Wise Men."

****

"Doctor," asked the patient, "do you think that I'll live to be a hundred?"

"Do you smoke or drink?" asked the doctor.

"No, doctor, never."

"Do you drive fast cars, gamble, or play around with wild women?"

"Of course, not!"

"Well, why do you want to live to be a hundred?" the doctor asked.

****

"I'd like to see an outtern."

"You mean an intern."

"Whatever you call him, I want a contamination."

"You mean an examination."

"I don't know what you call it, but I haven't demonstrated for months, and I'm stagnant."

Medico Mirth

While Tom was away at work, his wife decided to paint the toilet seat a bright, new colour. Then she went out shopping, not knowing that Tom would arrive home early, get short taken, and sit on the freshly-painted seat before it was dry.
When she returned, she found him stuck to the seat and yelling his head off. They tried and tried to no avail, but nothing would extract Tom's flesh from the seat. Finally, they unscrewed the toilet seat, and with a large overcoat covering Tom's predicament, they went for help to the doctor.
As they entered the doctor's surgery, Tom's wife pulled the coat aside and asked, "Doctor, have you ever seen anything like this?"
"Well," said the doctor, "I've seen many of them, but never have I seen one framed before."

****

A man went to the doctors complaining that he was disappointing his wife in bed. His whole performance was over in two minutes.
The doctor suggested that at the crucial moment he should give himself a shock, and that would do the trick. So on the way home, the man bought himself a starting pistol. When he got home, he found his wife already in bed. At the crucial moment of their lovemaking, he fired the starting pistol.
Next day he returned to the doctor's.
"How did it go?" the doctor asked.
"Jesus, doc, when I fired the pistol, my wife jumped up in shock, hit her head and landed in hospital with concussion, and the gas man came out of the wardrobe with his hands in the air!"

Muscle Bound Between the Ears (and blonde on top?)

You obviously come from the shallow end of the gene pool.

You're so dumb, even blondes tell jokes about you.

Two truckies come to a road under a bridge. A sign on the bridge says that the clearance height is twelve feet. One of the blokes gets out and measures the truck.
"Bugger! It's sixteen foot. We exceed the clearance by four foot. We'll have to back up and go a different road."
"What are y' talkin' about, mate?" asks the driver, revving the engine. "Get in, there's no coppers around. Who's goin' to know that we drove under th' flamin' bridge?"

****

Pickles was chuckling to himself at the bar.
"What's the joke?" asked the barman.
"The jokes on Stan. I've just learned that Stan is payin' my missus $20 to sleep with him, and she sleeps with me for nothing!"

****

The village idiot sat dangling a fishing line down a manhole. The new minister to the town gave him one dollar, and asked kindly, "How many have you caught today?"
"You be the tenth," he replied.

Muscle Bound Between the Ears (and blonde on top?)

"I came in answer to your ad for a handyman."
"Good, go and help lay some bricks."
"I'm sorry, I can't lay bricks."
"Then mix some concrete for the path."
"Sorry, can't mix concrete."
"Well, saw some wood, then."
"'Fraid I don't know how to saw."
"Tell me, what's so handy about you?"
"I just live around the corner."

****

People would often like to leave him with a thought, but he has no place to keep it.

****

A policeman came upon a man peeing in the park.
"Stop that immediately," he shouted, "and put it away!"
So the man did as he was told, but he couldn't stop himself from laughing.
"OK, what's so funny?" demanded the policeman.
"I fooled you, didn't I? I put it away," he laughed, "but I didn't stop."

****

"Mr Jones," said the judge, "I have listened very carefully to your case, and I've decided to award your wife $450 a month."
"Very generous of you, your honour," said Mr Jones. "I'll try and throw in a couple of quid meself every month."

Muscle Bound Between the Ears (and blonde on top?)

A man and his wife were on safari in darkest Africa. They were walking through the jungle when a huge lion jumped out in front of them, seized the wife in its jaws, and began dragging her off into the jungle.
"Shoot!" she screamed at her husband.
"I can't!" he cried. "I've run out of film!"

Merv Smith was working at the Kyneton meatworks when one of the machines went beserk and chopped off all his fingers. He dashed through the meatworks, out into the street, and ran two miles to the Kyneton Hospital.
He burst through the surgery door. Holding up his bloodied stumps, he cried, "Doctor, I've chopped off all me fingers. What can you do?"
"Good heavens!" cried the doctor. "Why didn't you bring your fingers with you? I could have stitched them back on!"
"I thought of that," said Merv, "but I couldn't pick them up!"

Muscle Bound Between the Ears (and blonde on top?)

A bloke was in a railway toilet block when he recognized the attendant. "G'day, Tom, I haven't seen you in years. What have you been doing?"

"I've been workin' here all the time," said the attendant.

"I bet you enjoy going on holidays."

"Holidays, what holidays?" asked Tom.

"You're entitled to four week's holidays for every year you've worked here. You should write to VicRail and tell them that you've been working here for twenty years without any holidays."

The attendant said he would do that.

When the bloke came back two weeks later, there was his mate in the toilet block, lying on a banana lounge. He was dressed in a floral shirt, shorts and thongs, and had a radio going at full blast beside him. He had a beer in one hand and a railway pie in the other.

"Did you write that letter I told you about?" asked the bloke.

"Yep. They sent me a lovely reply," said the attendant. "They apologized and said that I could take my holidays at MY OWN CONVENIENCE."

Muscle Bound Between the Ears (and blonde on top?)

A chemist employed a new girl and he left her in charge while he went to lunch. When he came back he asked how she went.

"A man came in and wanted some Colgate's toothpaste, but we didn't have any."

"Well, you should have suggested some Pepsodent, Macleans, or whatever else we had. Don't let that happen again. If we haven't got what they want, sell them something else."

The next day while the chemist was out to lunch, a man came in and asked for some toilet paper.

"Sorry," said the girl, "we're right out of toilet paper, but can I interest you in some wrapping paper, brown paper, fly paper, sandpaper, or confetti?"

****

A bloke went ice fishing. He bought himself a hammer, saw, stool, and a fishing rod. He bashed a hole in the ice with his hammer, and trimmed it with his saw. Then he sat down on his stool, and dropped the fishing rod down the hole. Suddenly a mighty voice boomed, "There are no fish down here!"

Trembling, he asked, "Is that you, God?"

"No," said the voice. "It's the manager of the ice skating rink."

Muscle Bound between the Ears (and blonde on top?)

A surgeon has just been included in the Guinness Book of Records. He is the first medico known to have separated a Siamese cat.

****

Three blokes were drowning their sorrows at the pub.
The first one said, "I think my wife's having an affair with a plumber. I came home yesterday to find the bedroom in a mess, and when I checked under the bed, there were a lot of pipes and wrenches."
"Know how you feel," said the second. "I think my wife's having an affair with an electrician. The bedroom was in a mess yesterday and when I checked under the bed, I found a tangled mess of insulation wires."
"My wife's doin' th' dirty on me, too. I reckon she's havin' an affair with a horse. When I came home yesterday the bedroom was all messed up, an' when I checked under the bed, I found a damned jockey!"

****

Why did the blonde stay up all night studying?
She had a urine test in the morning.

Did you hear about the blonde who was trapped in a shopping centre during a power failure?
She was trapped on the escalator for five hours!

Why don't blondes breastfeed their babies?
Because it hurts too much when they boil their nipples.

Muscle Bound Between the Ears (and blonde on top?)

Why does a blonde keep a coat hanger in the back seat of the car?
In case she locks her keys in the car.

What job does a blonde have in an M&M factory?
Proof reading.

How does a blonde turn on the light after she has had sex?
She opens the car door.

Why did the blonde fail her driver's licence test?
She wasn't used to being in the front seat.

What did the blonde do when the doctor told her she had sugar in her urine?
She peed on her Special K.

Why don't blondes eat jelly?
They can't work out how to get two cups of water into those little packages.

How do you get a blonde's eyes to twinkle?
Shine a torch into her ears.

Muscle Bound Between the Ears (and blonde on top?)

Three unemployed blondes were out shopping one day when they found an oil lamp in an antique store. When one of them rubbed it, a genie appeared. "I will grant you as much intelligence as you wish," said the genie.

"Fab!" said the first blonde. "I want to be ten times smarter than I am now," and in a flash the genie granted her wish. The next day she got a job as a teacher.

The second blonde said, "I think I'd like to be twenty times smarter," and in a flash, the genie granted her wish. The next day she got a job as a nuclear physicist.

Said the third blonde, "I like things the way they are. I don't have to go to work all the time … I think I'd like to be ten times dumber!"

Okey doke!" said the genie, and granted her wish.

Next day she woke up and found that she was a man.

****

A blonde came out of the kitchen, quite distraught. "Darling," she cried to her boyfriend, "I was just washing these ice cubes, and now they've disappeared!"

****

A blonde and a brunette are skydiving. The brunette jumps out of the plane, pulls the cord, and nothing happens. She pulls the emergency cord, but still nothing happens. Whereupon the blonde jumps out of the plane, yelling, "So, you want to race, do you?"

Muscle Bound Between the Ears (and blonde on top?)

What does a blonde say when she gives birth?
"Are you sure it's mine?"

A bloke was having a drink in a very dark bar. He leaned over to the very large woman alongside him and asked, "Wanna hear a blonde joke?"
"Well, yes," said the woman, "but I have to warn you – I'm six foot tall, weigh 120 kilos, and I'm a professional athlete and body builder. The blonde sitting next to me is six foot two, weighs 125 kilos, and is a professional wrestler, and next to her is another blonde who is six foot five, weighs 130 kilos, and is the current National Kick Boxing Champion. Now, do you still want to tell that joke?"
The bloke thought about it for a moment and said, "Nah, not if I have to tell it three times."

****

Three women are sitting in the waiting room of their gynaecologist.
The redhead says, "I think I'm going to have a boy because I was on top."
The brunette says, "Well, I think I'm going to have a girl because I was on the bottom."
With that, the blonde bursts into tears.
"I think I'm going to have puppies!" she sobs.

****

What do you call a blonde with two brain cells?
Pregnant.

Muscle Bound Between the Ears (and blonde on top?)

Two bored casino dealers are waiting for customers when in walks a very attractive blonde.
She wants to bet twenty thousand dollars on a single roll of the dice. She says to them, "I hope you don't mind, but I feel very lucky when I'm nude."
With that she strips naked and rolls the dice, while yelling, "Mama wants a new car!" Then she jumps up and down and starts hugging each dealer shouting, "Yes! Yes! I won! I won! Oh, thank you! Thank you!"
With that she picks up her money and clothes, and quickly leaves.
The dealers stare at each other, dumbfounded. Then one says, "Have you ever seen anything like that before?"
"Never," says the other, "by the way, did you see what she rolled?"
"No, I thought you did," says the first dealer.
MORAL OF THE STORY:- Not *all* blondes are dumb.

****

*H*ow do you keep a blonde busy all day long?
Put her in a round room and tell her to sit in the corner.

*W*hy did the blonde have tread-marks on her back?
From crawling across the street when the sign said, 'DON'T WALK.'

Naughty Naughties

Had more ins and outs than a showground turnstile

The Highland Games was in full swing with a lot of bagpipe playing, haggis eating and whisky sampling. As the day progressed, those sampling whisky in the sponsor's tent became increasingly inebriated.
One woman became wildly enamoured of Jock.
"Jock, have you anything up your kilt?" she asked.
"Put your hand up and find out," he said.
Without hesitation, she did just that.
"Oh, Jock," she cried, shocked. "It's gruesome!"
"Put your hand up there again," said Jock, "and it will grew some more."

****

A bloke picked up a girl in a bar and took her home. After some preliminary drinks, they got undressed and got into bed. After a few minutes, the girl started laughing. A bit put out, the bloke asked her what she found so amusing.
"Your organ," she laughed, "It's a bit on the small side."
"Well," he replied, "it's not used to playing in cathedrals."

****

A bloke walks into a petrol station and buys a packet of cigarettes. He pulls one out and starts smoking.
"I'm sorry, sir," says the attendant, "but you can't smoke in here."
"Don't you think it's stupid if I can *buy* them here, but I can't *smoke* them here?"
"No, I don't, because we also sell condoms!"

Naughty Naughties

*H*umpty Dumpty didn't fall off the wall – he took his sheila up and knocked her off!

*D*oggie position is popular:
  Man sits up and begs,
  Wife lies down and goes to sleep.

*C*onfucius says, "Man who goes through airport turnstile sideways is going to Bangkok."

*B*umper *S*tickers:
IF YOU DRINK, DON'T PARK – ACCIDENTS CAUSE PEOPLE

IF THAT PHONE WAS UP YOUR ARSE, MAYBE YOU COULD DRIVE A LITTLE BETTER

CONSTIPATED PEOPLE DON'T GIVE A SHIT

IMPOTENCE: NATURE'S WAY OF SAYING 'NO HARD FEELINGS'

****

*H*ow do you know that Santa Claus doesn't have any kids? Because he only comes once a year, and then it's down the chimney.

*W*hy can't Frankenstein have any kids? Because his nuts are on his neck.

Naughty Naughties

Imagine if major companies started producing or sponsoring condoms. Imagine the advertising and trademarks –
Toyota Condoms: Oh…what a feeling!
Ford Condoms: The ride of your life.
KFC Condoms: Finger lickin' good.
M & M Condoms: They melt in your mouth, not in your hands.
Coca-Cola Condoms: It's the real thing.
Eveready Condoms: Keeps going and going…..
Macintosh Condoms: It does more, it costs less, it's that simple.
Microsoft Condoms: Where do you want to go today?
Pringles Condoms: Once you pop, you can't stop

****

A widow is feeling a bit lonely, so she puts an ad in the paper, "Woman seeking a man who is good in bed, won't abuse her, and won't run away."
Weeks pass, but one day her doorbell rings. When she opens the door, she sees a man with no arms, no legs, and sitting in a wheelchair.
"My name is Alf. I'm here in answer to your advert, love. I've got to tell you, without a doubt, I'm your man."
"Oh, yes," says the widow suspiciously, "what makes you think that?"
"Well," Alf smiles, "I have no arms so I can't abuse you, and I have no legs so I can't run away."
"But," says the widow, rolling her eyes, "how do I know that you're good in bed?"
Alf smirks, "How do you think I rang your doorbell?"

Naughty Naughties

When Harry came home from work, his wife told him that they had been invited to a fancy dress party that weekend. After thinking about a costume for a while, they decided to go as Adam and Eve.
Harry contacted the Costume Hire shop, and ordered the kind of fig leaf that would do the job. When it arrived, it was far too small, so he sent it back and asked for a larger one. However, after several attempts, it didn't seem possible to get a fig leaf large enough to cover what Harry had to hide.
Finally, Harry sent a message, "Please send the largest fig leaf you have."
Back came the answer, "Sorry, we can't help you. Suggest you stick it in your ear and go as a petrol pump."

****

Jake the plumber was on a house job. By mid afternoon he and the lady of the house were having a tumble in the bedroom when the phone rang.
"That's my husband. He is coming home now because he's got a meeting tonight. Why don't you come back tonight and we'll take up where we left off?"
"What?" said the plumber. "On my own time?"

****

She's seen more ceilings than Michelangelo.

He's sown enough wild oats for us to call him Uncle Toby.

"I love younger men," she said. "They mightn't know what they're doing, but they can do it all night."

Naughty Naughties

Being seduced is a matter of perfect timing. The woman has to give in just before the man gives up.

****

What's the definition of trust?
Two cannibals giving each other a blow job.

****

My brother hates daylight saving. He gets his early morning erection on the 8.30 train to the office.

****

The truckie stopped at a new diner in the middle of the desert. He fronted up to the counter, and asked for two hamburgers and a hot dog.
He saw the female assistant go to the fridge, reach for two rissoles and whack one up under each armpit.
"Hang on, what's the big idea?" asked the truckie.
"Everything is deep frozen out here, luv," said the assistant. "That's the only way I can thaw them out."
"Well, okay," said the truckie, "but cancel the hot dog."

****

A young bloke had the hots for his new girlfriend, but he was ashamed of his small penis.
One dark night in the back seat of his car, he finally got up the nerve to put it in her hand.
"No thanks," she said, "I don't smoke."

****

Laugh, and the world laughs with you. Cry, and you're probably looking at your penis.

Naughty Naughties

It was a very expensive brothel, but he was surprised to find all the women looked like his mother. They sat in a line, in chenille dressing-gowns, fluffy slippers, and their hair in curlers.
The Madam explained, "We specialize here in clients who suffer from premature ejaculation."

Two blokes were ambling along the footpath when a stunning young woman walked towards them. She had a great figure, beautiful face, and a magnificent head of bright red hair. As she passed them, they were enveloped in a cloud of intoxicating perfume.
One bloke turned to the other, and asked, "Hey mate, have you ever slept with a gorgeous bluey like that?"
"Nah," said the other, "not a bloody wink."

****

A couple were lying in bed after a bout of lovemaking, when she said dreamily, "If I'm pregnant and we have a baby, what will we call him?"
The bloke ripped off his condom, tied it in a knot, and chucked it out the window. "If he gets out of that, we'll call him Houdini."

Naughty Naughties

One night as a couple lay in bed, the husband gently tapped his wife on the shoulder, and started rubbing her arm.
"I'm sorry, sweetheart," she said, "but I have an appointment with my gynaecologist tomorrow, and I want to stay fresh."
The husband, rejected, turned over and tried to sleep.
A few minutes later he turned back to her, put his hand on her breast and whispered in her ear, "Do you have a dentist appointment, as well?"

****

Tom had worked in a pickle factory for a number of years when one day he came home and confessed to his wife that he had a terrible urge to stick his penis into the pickle slicer.
His wife suggested that he should see a sex therapist, but he declined, saying that he was too embarrassed to do so. He vowed that he'd beat the compulsion on his own.
A few weeks later he came home in a terrible state.
"What's wrong, Tom?" asked his wife, terribly concerned.
"Do you remember how I told you that I had this tremendous urge to put my penis in the pickle slicer?"
"Oh, Tom, you didn't."
"Yes, I did."
"My God, what happened?"
"I got fired."
"No, Tom. I mean, what happened to the pickle slicer?
"Oh...she got fired, too."

****

Eunuch? *A man who has had his works cut out for him.*

Naughty Naughties

As the airliner pushed back from the gate, the flight attendant gave the passengers the usual information regarding seat belts, etc. Finally she said, "Now sit back and enjoy your trip while your captain, Judith Campbell, and crew take you safely to your destination."
Joe, sitting in the eight row, thought to himself, "Did I hear right? Is the captain a woman?" When the attendant came by with the drink cart, he asked, "Did I understand you right? Is the captain a woman?"
"Yes," said the attendant, "the entire crew is female."
"My God," said Joe, "I'd better have two scotch and sodas! I don't know what to think of all those women up there in the cockpit."
"That's another thing, sir," said the attendant, "we no longer call it a cockpit ... Now it's a box office."

****

The prostitute was protesting to the police that she was not selling sex. "I am just selling condoms for a hundred dollars each, and I simply give a free demonstration on how to use them," she said.

****

My wife can't wrestle, but you oughta see her box!"

****

"I wonder what people would say if they could see me here on this beach absolutely starkers."
"They'd say I married you for your money," said his wife.

Naughty Naughties

His father was alarmed when he announced that he was going to marry Miss Lottsabazooma.
"Son," he said, "Everybody in town has been to bed with her."
The son thought about this for a moment.
"Yeah, but it's not a very big town, is it?"

****

The young couple had a knee-trembler against a paling fence, and in their excitement, they knocked the fence down. The commotion aroused the householder, who grabbed the young man and collected one hundred dollars on the spot for repairs.
Later the bloke said, "Sally, you're a feminist and always shouting about equal rights. Here's your chance. You owe me fifty dollars for half the cost of the fence."
"No way," said Sally, "you did all the pushing."

****

May you live as long as you want to, and want to as long as you live.

Old Codgers

*S*o old that when he was born his family tree was just a sapling.

*S*o old that her birthday cake looked like a bushfire.

A ninety-year-old man booked into a posh hotel to celebrate his birthday. As a special surprise, some friends sent a call girl to his room. When he opened the door, the beautiful, young woman cooed, "I have a present for you. I'm here to give you super sex."
"Thanks very much," said the old bloke thoughtfully, "I'll have soup."

*N*inety-two-year-old Ethel comes into the dayroom of the nursing home with her fist clenched. As she raises her hand into the air, she announces, "Anyone who can guess what I have in my hand can have sex with me tonight!"
After a long silence, one old bloke sighs, "It's an elephant."
"Close enough, sweetheart!" Ethel purrs.

****

*W*hen he was young, his heart ruled his head. When he was middle-aged, his head ruled his heart. Now that he's 65, his bladder rules both!

Old Codgers

An old bloke shuffles into the doctor's surgery in great pain. He's very embarrassed, but he tells the doctor that his penis is very sore and tender.
"It's the missus," he says, "Y'see, last night she dreamt she was playing the pokies and my old fella was the lever."
"Good heavens!" says the doctor, "Why didn't you say something?"
"I couldn't, doc. I had a mouthful of ten cent pieces!"

****

Three old ladies were walking through the park when a man jumped out from behind a tree and flashed at them. Two of them had strokes, but the third wasn't fast enough.

****

An old man sat looking at his manhood. Sighing, he said, "Well, old friend, here we are. We were born together, grew up together, and we married together. But now, after all these years, why did you have to die before me?"

****

The old man hobbled into the doctor's surgery. He was very agitated.
"Oh, doctor, you've got to give me something to lower my sex drive."
"Now, hang on Mr Stevens, it's all in your head, you know."
"That's right! That's what I mean – you've got to lower it a bit."

Old Codgers

Two old men were sitting on a park bench outside the local town hall where a flower show was in progress.
"Cripes," said one, "life is boring. We never seem to have any fun these days. For two bucks I'd take off my gear and streak through the flower show."
"You're on!" said the other old bloke, holding up two dollars.
The first bloke struggled out of his clothes as fast as he could and, completely naked, streaked through the front door of the Town Hall.
Waiting outside, his friend heard a huge commotion inside the hall, followed by great applause. The naked old man burst out through the door surrounded by a cheering crowd. "How did you go?" asked the friend.
"Good-oh!" said the streaker. "I won first prize as a dried arrangement!"

You know you're getting old when you don't have an enemy in the world – they're all dead.

****

It's a fact that at 80, there are six women for every man. What a great time in life to get odds like that!

Old Codgers

Tom O'Dwyer was ninety years old, but he still managed to go to confession every Sunday, although it took him 15 minutes to struggle up the aisle.
This Sunday after he entered the confessional he said, "Bless me Father, for I have sinned. I committed adultery with an 18-year-old lass."
"My goodness!" exclaimed the priest, hardly able to believe his ears. "When did this happen?"
"About 60 years ago, Father, but I felt like cheering myself up with some nice thoughts."

Two old ladies were on holiday, and were visiting the Roman Room in the British Museum. In the centre was a magnificent statue of a Roman God, naked except for a fig leaf. After looking at it Joyce wandered on, but suddenly realized that Emma wasn't with her.
"Hey, Emma!" she called, spotting her friend beneath the statue. "What are you waiting for, Christmas?"
"No," Joyce replied, "autumn."

Old Codgers

Old George was almost 85, and as he wasn't feeling well, his wife took him to the doctor.
He was a bit Mutt and Jeff, and so his missus would answer most of the questions for him.
As the doctor was examining him, the doctor said, "You're not doing bad for your age."
"What did he say?" asked George.
"You're not bad for your age, you silly old bugger!" she yelled at him.
"What are his symptoms?" asked the doctor.
"He finds it painful to go to the toilet," she told him.
"I'm going to need some samples of his urine, stools and semen, if possible," said the doctor. "Can you manage that?"
"What'd he say?" George yelled at his missus.
"He said he wants to examine your pyjamas!" she yelled back.

****

A little old man sits on the pavement outside a mutinational corporation selling shoelaces at 20 cents a pair. Every day at 5.30 the CEO of the company leaves the building, and gets into his chauffeur-driven Rolls Royce. However, before he does, he always goes over to the old man, puts 20 cents on his tray, but never takes the laces. This goes on for 20 years without either of them speaking a word.
Then one day after the CEO has put the 20 cents on the old man's tray and is getting into the Rolls, he hears the old man call him. He looks around, and the old man is beckoning him over. He hesitates, goes back and bends down to hear what he has to say.
The old man looks up at him. "They've gone up."

Pissed as a Parrot

So full he'd even try drinking spiked heels and a nip in the air

A young athlete was doing push-ups in the park when a drunk went past, and then came back and laughed hysterically. "What's so funny?" asked the athlete indignantly.
"I hate to tell you thish, mate," said the drunk, "but your girlfriend's gone home!"

****

A drunk staggered into a police station, and complained, "Someone's been in my car, and they've stolen the steering wheel, the brake, the clutch, the pedals – bloody everything!"
Seeing that the man was so drunk, the policeman humoured him for a few minutes, and then said he'd come and investigate after he'd made a few phone calls. Meanwhile, the drunk staggered outside, but came back five minutes later. "Don't bother, officer," he said. "S' alright, my mistake. I got into the back seat."

****

What's the difference between a toilet and a barman?
A toilet only has to deal with one arsehole at a time.

****

"What do you drink?"
"Whisky and carrot juice."
"That's a weird combination."
"Well, you get drunk just as fast, but you can see where you're going to fall."

Pissed as a Parrot

A group of wine buffs were gathered around a bar drinking various wines, and demonstrating their ability to identify them. A slightly inebriated bloke stepped forward and challenged them to identify wines while blindfolded. The challenge was taken up by the champion wine taster of the group. After tasting the first wine, he said, "It's a Rhinelander, Cabernet Sauvignon."
"Yes, but what year?" asked the inebriated one.
"I think," he sipped, "it's 1955."
His friends cheered him on to the next challenge.
"It's a Tuscan Shiraz."
"What year?"
"I believe it's a 1968."
While the group cheered their champion, the challenger staggered from the room and returned with another glass. This one proved more difficult to name. He sipped, then suddenly spat it out and ripped off the blindfold. "Good lord!" he exclaimed, "This isn't wine, at all, it's plain urine!"
"That's right," replied the drunk, "but how old am I?"

****

"William Arnold Smith, you are up before the bench today because of alcohol," said the judge. "Alcohol has caused you to be in this predicament."
"Oh, thanks, your honour. Everyone else said it was my fault."

****

Drunk? He once stuck 20 cents in the parking meter, and when the dial went to 60, he said, "Jesus! I weigh one hour!"

Pissed as a Parrot

A drunk was staggering along the street behind a woman shopper when she dropped a parcel. When she was out of sight, he picked it up and found that it was full of sausages. In case she should come back, he shoved the parcel down the front of his trousers and made his way to the bus stop. Once on the bus, he began to feel hungry, so he opened the front of his trousers, pulled out a sausage, and cut off a piece with his pocket knife. A woman sitting opposite him fainted.

A little bit later, he pulled out another sausage from his trousers, cut off a piece of it, and another woman fainted. He was still hungry, so he pulled out another, cut off a piece of it, and HE fainted!

****

A man with no arms went into a bar and ordered a pint of beer. When it arrived, he asked the barman if he'd mind reaching over and getting the money out of his trouser pocket. When the barman obliged, he asked if he'd also mind holding the glass up to his lips. The barman obliged. "It must be difficult, having no arms," said the barman. "It sure is," the bloke nodded. "It is quite embarrassing, too, at times. By the way, could you tell me where the gents is, please?"

The barman hesitated. "Sure, mate, a couple of miles down the road, on the right."

Pissed as a Parrot

When the policeman saw O'Connell fumbling with a front door lock, and then forcing a front window of a house, he became suspicious. He put his heavy hand on his collar, just as O'Connell was halfway through the window.
"But ish my house, offisher," O'Connell protested, and invited the policeman in to prove it.
"There y'are, thash my cat, thash my armchair, thish is my bedroom, thash my wife in bed, and that bloke with her, thash me."

****

Bill woke his wife. "'Ish a miracle," he said. "You wouldn't believe it, Mavis, but I just went for a leak, and the light came on by itself. Didn't touch the switch. Had a leak, an' ash soon as I left, the light went out – all by itself. Untouched by human hands. Ish a miracle, I tell ya."
His wife sighed. "For God's sake, get into bed, Bill. You've pissed in the fridge again."

Pissed as a Parrot

A policeman sees a car weaving all over the road, and so he pulls it over. As he confronts the woman driver, he can smell alcohol on her breath.
"I'm going to give you a breathalyzer test to see if you are over the limit for driving under the influence of alcohol." She blows into the bag, and the policeman walks back to the police car. On returning, he says, "It looks like you've had a couple of stiff ones."
"Goodness, officer, you mean it shows that, too?"

****

The fire engine careered around the corner, and whizzed off down the road, its bell clanging, just after a drunk staggered out of the pub. He promptly chased after it, weaving down the road, until he collapsed, exhausted and weeping.
"All right," he sobbed, "you can keep your bloody ice-creams!"

****

Mick and Clarrie got drunk and went fishing. They hadn't been fishing long when they pulled out a bottle with a genie inside. The genie said that he would grant them one wish.
Mick said, "I wish all thish water around the boat was beer."
Immediately the whole lake turned to beer.
"You've really gone and done it," said Clarrie, "Now we'll have to piss in the boat!"

Pissed as a Parrot

Murphy stumbled out of the pub one night, and sat down on the curb under a lamp post. While urinating he fell asleep, and two pranksters came along and tied a blue ribbon around his penis.

When he woke next morning, he said to his old fella, "I don't know where you've been or what you've been doing, but I'm glad to see you won first prize."

****

At three o'clock in the morning a bedraggled man in a pink negligee staggered up to the hotel desk.

"Is there something I can do for you?" the night clerk asked.

"Yesh," said the man,"I wanna be shown up to room 205 on the secon' floor.

"I'm sorry," said the clerk, "that room is occupied by a Mr Brendan O'Dwyer. Mr O'Dwyer has that room."

"Thass it. Thass the room."

"I'm sorry," repeated the clerk, "but I can't disturb Mr O'Dwyer at this time of night unless it's absolutely urgent."

"Lishen, I don't want any more sass outa you. I wanna be shown up to room 205."

"Perhaps you have a message for the occupant."

"Neva mind if I have a messhidge or not."

"Then, could I have your name?"

"My name ish Brendan O'Dwyer, an' I jush fell out o' room 205 about five minutes ago."

Tight-arses

So cheap he'd tell his kids that Santa died in a car crash on Christmas Eve

On a Sunday drive he'd make his missus push to save petrol.

A couple were worried about the amount of money they had been spending, so they decided to adopt a savings plan. The husband said that every time they had sex, he'd put $20 in the piggy bank.
Around a year later, the husband decided to empty the piggy bank.
"I've been putting $20 notes in here every time we have sex, yet there are $50 and $100 notes, as well!" he shrieked. "What's been going on?"
His wife sniffed, "Not everyone's as cheap as you!"

****

Sandy began to be a little deaf, but he was too tight to buy a hearing aid. So he scrounged some thin wire, and put one end in his pocket and the other end behind his ear. It made no difference to his deafness, but it encouraged everyone to speak louder to him.

****

When a millionaire in his eighties decided to marry an eighteen year old chorus girl, the vicar protested.
"I don't believe in marrying for money."
"Good," replied the millionaire, "then I won't insult you by offering you a fee for performing the ceremony."

Tight-arses

A married couple's bank account has fallen into the red, and they have two weeks to redress the issue. They also receive a final notice from the electricity company. They agree to save money right away. That evening, however, the husband puts on his coat and says, "I'm off down the pub."
"How dare you?" screams his wife, "haven't we just agreed to go on a strict budget?"
The husband nods and tells his wife to put on her warmest coat.
"But why? Are we going out together?" she asks.
"No, but I'm turning the heating off."

****

This bloke was at a friend's funeral when one of the mourners remembered he owed the deceased $10. So he said, "I am a man of my word," and put a $10 note in the coffin.
His action reminded another mourner of a debt that he owed the deceased, and so he put another $10 in the coffin.
"You two have pricked my conscience," said the bloke, and so he came forward, wrote out a cheque for $30, and took $20 change.

****

He gave the waiter a tip, but it didn't even run a place.

When the police put a price on his head, he turned himself in.

Tight-arses

An old tight-wad was sitting by his wife's bed. She was desperately ill, and had little time to live.
"Alice," he whispered, "I've got to get down to the post office to collect my pension. If you feel yourself going before I get back, will you switch the light off?"

****

Two tight-arsed men, Bill and Harry, were on a mountaineering holiday in New Zealand when Bill slipped and fell, and ended up hanging by his fingertips over a crevasse.
"Quick, Harry," he screamed, "get down to the village and buy a rope. I don't know how long I can hang on here!"
Harry raced off down the mountain, and after twenty minutes had passed, Bill's grip was beginning to weaken. Then, to his relief, he heard Harry returning.
"Hurry up, help me, quick!" yelled Bill. "Have you got the rope?"
"No," said Harry, "those greedy buggers wanted $10 for it."

Tight-arses

A tight-arse is a person whose thrift teaches him to take long steps to save shoe leather, but whose caution advises him to take short steps to avoid ripping his pants.

****

The wristwatch was invented by a tight-arse who objected to taking anything out of his pocket.

****

He's such a tight-fisted wanker that he has blisters on his willy.

****

Ted was due for his annual medical check-up, and arrived, as usual, with a very liberal specimen in a very large bottle. After the test, the doctor announced that there was nothing abnormal in the specimen, and that Ted was fine.
He returned home happily to his family to tell them the good news.
"Betty," he smiled, "you and I, the kids and grandma are all in good health."

****

He's so mean he eats baked beans for supper so that he can enjoy a bubble bath the next day.

Tin Lids

Mum took one look at me when I was born and said to Dad, "What will we call it?"
He said, "Quits!"

One Monday morning, two lawyers were discussing their weekends.
"I got a dog for my kids," said one.
"Good trade," replied the other lawyer.

****

After finding her daughter playing doctors with the neighbour's son, an irate mother strode across the street to confront his parents.
"Don't take it too seriously," said the kid's mother. "It's only natural for children their age to want to satisfy their curiosity."
"Curiosity!" the girl's mother bellowed. "He removed her appendix!"

****

A city boy was sent to the country to spend a holiday on his uncle's farm. When he returned home he was bubbling over with news of everything he'd seen. His mum asked him to name all his uncle's animals. "Well, I saw horses and pigs and some bulls and cows and some fuckers."
"Some fuckers?" asked his mother.
"Well, Uncle Harry called them 'eifers, but I knew what he meant."

****

We were so poor as kids that the only time we had meat was when we bit our tongues.

Tin Lids

"Why are you looking so down in the mouth, today?" asked Tommy's geography teacher.
"I didn't have any breakfast this morning," mumbled Tommy.
"You poor thing," said the teacher. "Never mind, let's get on with the lesson. Tommy, where is the French border?"
"In bed with my Mum," said Tommy. "That's why I didn't get any breakfast!"

****

When a schoolteacher comes into the classroom one morning, she finds a lovely red apple on the desk with a note next to it that says, "From the Italian kids."
"How sweet!" says the teacher.
Next day she finds a lovely ripe pear on her desk with a note that says, "From the Greek kids."
"How sweet!" the teacher says.
The third day she finds a lovely, firm banana on her desk, but when she reads the note beside it, she blushes bright red.
"Who's responsible for this? Come on – own up! Who put this on my desk?"
A little black boy stands up. "Please, miss, I thought you'd like a banana …."
"I'm not talking about the banana!" snaps the teacher.
"I'm talking about the foul, disgusting note that came with it. I'm surprised at you. A boy of your age shouldn't use such filthy language. Do you know what it means?"
"Yes, miss," says the little black boy. "It stands for From Us Coloured Kids."

Tin Lids

One night the young boy's mother took him and his elderly grandmother out to tea at a restaurant.
Halfway through the meal the little boy whispered to his mother that he needed to go to the toilet.
"O.K, dear," said his mother. "I'll take you in a minute."
"No, I want grandma to take me," said the little boy.
"Why, what's so special about grandma?" asked his mother.
"Well," said the boy, "Her hand shakes …"

****

A young boy was approached by the young housewife who had just moved in to the flat next door. "Sonny, I need some bread from the corner store. Do you think you could go for me?"
"No," said the boy, "but I heard my Dad say he could."

****

"**D**ad, is it true we're descended from monkeys?"
"Dunno, son. I never met any of your mother's relations."

Tin Lids

Mrs Jones was preparing dinner when little Tony came in. "And what has Mummy's darling been doing outside?" she asked.
"I've been playing postman," said Tony.
"Postman?" asked his mother. "How could you do that without any letters to deliver?"
"I had lots of letters," said Tony. "I found them in an old box in the garage, all tied up with pink ribbons. I put one in every letterbox in the street."

A teacher is reminding her class of tomorrow's big exam. "Now, students, I won't accept any excuses for not attending school tomorrow. It is a very important exam."
"But what if it's a really, really good excuse?" asks one girl.
"Well, if it's a national disaster, a critical illness, a death in the family, or something like that. But that's it."
The class smart-arse puts his hand up, and says,
"What would you say tomorrow if I said I was suffering from complete and utter sexual exhaustion?"
The class snickers.
When silence is restored, the teacher says, "Well, I guess you'll have to write your exam with the other hand."

www.ingramcontent.com/pod-product-compliance
Lightning Source LLC
Chambersburg PA
CBHW050319010526
44107CB00055B/2311